CW00871711

We Are Going Home

We Are Going Home

Annie

Library of Congress Control Number: 2018907239
ISBN: Hardcover   978-1-9845-3594-8
               Softcover   978-1-9845-3595-5
               eBook   978-1-9845-3596-2

Print information available on the last page.

Rev. date: 06/20/2018

To order additional copies of this book, contact:
Xlibris
1-888-795-4274
www.Xlibris.com
Orders@Xlibris.com
771938

CONTENTS

"Growing Up In Mangry in the western islands"

Moving to Mangry in the western islands Fagaloa was a little bit of change there. I learn certain stuffs from my family, relatives, and also my eldest siblings. I was a little girl at the time and I don't understand why everything changes little by little. Anyways, I moved to Mangry in the western islands, I see tons of people that have faith in God. I was born in Western islands, and all my life was a Catholic, and I was a part of the service in the church when I was little. And also I was involve in the secret committee during that time. At that time, I couldn't understand the way I believe and how things work out. Evil comes in my family, and the first thing that came up to mind was, "why is he doing this?, why is he scaring me and not others?". At the same time, I have seen tons of people coming to Mangry in the western islands Fagaloa village and try to stand a

new church but too late the catholic is already there. I love my people and my village, and the reason why, it's because my people look after each other, and take care of each other. And the most awesome thing is that they all respect Sunday, because that's the day we worship and praise our Father God all as one and of course it's our Holy day. We prepare everything before Sabbath, and when it's Sunday, all the church families feed or serve the pastor. Every day I cook, but before I serve the food for my family, I make the pastors food first and I go deliver it to his house. Days go by, and finally I see happiness in my village. They don't worry about food, money, or anything. We plant our own food like banana, taro, papaya, bread fruit, mango, guava, and orange.

"Our Living Life Without Silverware"

Living together with my family gives me happiness. One day ive seen my family for the first time, and realize everything and there meaning, and to get me to the point where I am going to stay with my mom's family. I saw my mom leaving with her husband and I was a little confused about what's going on and why my mom wants me to stay with her family. I stayed at Orchidand Joseph Andrew Marigold's land. I love the way people look after each other and respect others. People help without paying. Back in the days during my time, we work for others and help others for free. We believe and trust in God, that's why whatever we do, we do it from the bottom of my heart, and God will pay you back. Living our life back in the days with no silverware was a happy life. When we cook food we dig the ground and it that hole we dig, we make our food in there. And we cook it in the Samoan way. Before the typhoon destroys our country, I see the love and the beauty of the

land that it was before. I saw my grandparents working hard and trying their best to help the people of the village, and also to help our church people and everybody. During that time, that's when I saw my grandfather leads lots of position in the village and also he loves them like his own. My grandfather is a fisher man and also he's a farmer man. At the age of 6, that is when I started to see things. Just like what I mention before about the typhoon destroying our village, not only our village but the whole South Pacific Ocean. I've seen a lots of people that have no place to stay, but lucky thing all the church people and the people from outside the village we all went and stay in the Catholic church. I don't remember how long the typhoon has been gone, and finally the help from the Unites State and from the around the world has arrived. But before that help arrived, we don't have any candles to make a light neither fresh food. All the high chiefs of the village help a lot of people. They help and serve people with whatever they can afford. But now days, I don't know what to say. After the typhoon we celebrate a birthday. I don't remember whose birthday was is but it was on a moon light. After our dinner, my cousins went and play hide and seek. So that night, I decided to go and sit on the fifth floor of our house. While I was sitting on the fifth floor, I said, "Come out now". After I said that I saw a short man wearing a black suit with one light on his forehead. I saw him walking from the where we shower at. But I wasn't afraid. I saw him walking to the shack and end up running to where I am sitting at. His on the ground standing on the sand but I was sitting on the fifth floor of our house. He throws sands at me and I did the same

thing by throwing him back with the sands. No one in my family saw him only me. I call my family to come and see this short man, but when my family came out of the house he disappears out of nowhere and my family thinks that I was lying to them and didn't trust me at all. But only God knows the truth. I saw that short man and I believe that he came from under the water. But before he disappear, I look down at him from where I was sitting at and waved at him, and he also waved back at me. After I saw this short man, I become not too scared or afraid. Whatever was happen in my life by then, I feel some power in me to fight for my life. The evil came and destroy my body and make me feel ugly and dirty. I know God makes me go through that because it always comes to me. I see my family loved me, and take care of me. I know no one was born to be suffered. Everybody was born to be happy and enjoy the freedom and last is to live peace from the Lord. Year by year and started to see changes. Opposite of happiness is fight, and I saw foundation of our village is change. Law has been change, people change. People act that they have money and act rich but doesn't have a heart to help other that are in needs. I see the happiness and rich life, and I picked happy life. Why? Because I know I was still a young girl and I like playing with happy kids, and playing with them makes me happy too. I always honor and plus I am the only little girl that always spoil no matter what people say. I am the only little girl in my family that is not scared at all. My family knows that I am the only person that knows all about my grandparents, because I was with them until my mother came and took me away from them. I was happy when I

saw my coming but sad at the same time because I see my grandparents crying already. When I was about to leave with my mom, my grandparents said to me, "you know where we at if you want to come back". I enjoy staying with my grandparents Orchidand Utal Philips Utal. There life when I was a little girl, every day they serve the pastors and their family, and then the elders second together with the high chiefs of the village. You know all the blessings are from those small villages, even Cosmic Village too. The chiefs and I tap hands and they thank me for serving them. I knew all these things before I have my kids and grandbabies. The life before was leading with the power of love, and I never thought about losing or fail. The teaching before is still calling me. What I mean is to prepare our life form from before. I saw everything my people teach me. Respect is the power, and caring with love. It was a happy life. Thinking I was young and no one knows the truth of my life. They just use me and say that I'm their daughter but she doesn't know anything. I know that you're thinking is right but to me, you're wrong. Why I say wrong, because no one in this world would treat their kids in that type of way. What I do I run away from them because I want to be free? Looking at the hard life, it likes a magic to someone from a low life. I want to imagine that modern kind of life we need now. Free from everything. The only purpose that my family was focusing on was their happiness and their life. I've seen a lots of my families passed away in their own peaceful moment. In my country, whenever a family have funeral, the whole village cry themselves out and they will all help each other. Look at the point of our life. My point

is, love is better than anything. When it's Sunday, the entire family member goes to church the only person that stays home is the one that's preparing food and everything. Plus if anyone or someone don't obey the elders and show respect, it's a must for you to obey them. The kind of happiness that I have is no fear, no lie, and no strangers. My family is my home. I know and I believe that there is no place like home. No matter what happen in my life, I know that I have to get all my life together and write it down. It is the idea from the spirit of our God, and I know that it a must to do I to sacrifice all of us. It's a long journey to Heaven. We must return and hear him. I know our time is not God's time. The most awesome thing I love my people is that they welcome everyone. They teach their kids base in the bible. Every day before then, we all go to our priest's house for our bible school. Our mother, which is the priests wife, she is the one the teaches us how to write and how to write own Samoan alphabet (A, E, I,O, U, F, G, L, M, N, P, S, T, U, V). That is our samoan alphabet that John William wrote. And he is the one who wrote the first manuscript of my country. I enjoyed my young life with tons of powerful people. I saw a man before, he was talking to himself while walking, and I know people disappear by then. I heard lots of stories about short people. But it is true and I know one day that cave will open. My grandfather was telling story, and everybody was talking about a men that went fishing, and he got a red fish. That red fish told the man to leave the ocean and go home, but I will wait for you on the mountain tomorrow morning. What I'm saying is based on a true story. On the next day, this man took his dog with him on

the mountain, and while there on their way up the mountain the dog found a pig. That pig ran inside the cave and so the dog decided to follow the pig. This man was calling his dog to come out but the dog couldn't hear him. So the was just standing in from of the cave and continue to call the dog. So, finally the dog came out of the cave and he was covered with sands. Then the dog's owner was trying to ask his dog what was down there, but the dog ran back inside and wanted his owner to follow him. But the dog's owner thinks that it not safe for him. Finally he decided to enter the cave.

The dog's owner finally joins his dog in the cave and kept going until they hear voices of people talking. When they got to where the voices are coming from, they saw a big huge family of God under the cave. So this poor man and the family of God make and agreement. And after they make the agreement the poor man came out of the cave. When he got back, the village ask him where was he at, and he told the village about what he saw in the cave. But the agreement they make was to not let anyone know what's inside or under the cave. Once this poor man told the village about it, everything that he had has disappeared. I told my grandfather about everything is changing, and my grandfather said, "God I know one day you will do your will as soon as possible". Everything changes so badly. The bad thing I saw was families were fighting, village against other villages, and kids disrespecting their parents and telling lies in front of their faces. All this is happening because of the typhoon. I know everything is coming through hard way and people are hard to understand. Why? It's because when you ask your son or daughter with what you need and they say to leave them alone. And I am sorry to say that. During my time, I am a respectful person. No matter your old or young, I will always honor to serve you with all my heart, because I want to show people the kind of person I am. I remember the school that I was in, it different from what my grandmother has taught me. And from there, I always remember her face, her lovely smile and her kindness. Thinking about that smile and the way she teaches me, makes me feel believe that we've got to bring that life back.

"Life Was Like Heaven"

Before, our life was fresh. We eat fresh food every day.
The lives of no worry, no fear, no store, nothing, only fresh
food and fresh pure water to drink. Life changes by growing
up in different direction, meeting new people that you have
never seen before. God make me move and make me serve
other. Staying with family you don't know, it's really hard.
First, when you ask for your needs they just ignore. The first
family that I stayed with was my uncle Philips's girlfriend
house. The only people at the house were the mom, dad,
and the little sister. They left me there and make other
people watch me. I was sad when I was with them. Why?
because they use me as their water runner. I remember
when I got pink eye, they didn't even care. I was in pain
and crying because I want to go back home, but I was too
scared to tell them. And I don't know the way back home
to my family. Every day when I sleep, I just want to sleep
and never wake up. I was lost and hurt, and those are the

things that I could never forget. The way these family treat me doesn't match with the way that I grew up with. I was crying one morning, and I saw a bus coming to the house, and I know that I am going back home. My grandma saw me crying but she can't say nothing because she respect what my grandfather told her.

"End Up Staying With My Sister In Fa'atoia"

I went back to my grandparents' house and stay there for a while, and my families were planning to go visit my other uncle at the other village called Two Way House Villages in Western Islands. I was counting days for us to go. So we went to Falelili to visit my uncle, and end up my grandmother agree for me to stay there in Saleilua, until she come back and get me with my two cousins. We were so happy to stay there. Lots of things happen there. My cousin Tina got married there and my grandparents still didn't come and get us. One day while I was walking on the street, I saw a pick-up truck coming but I didn't stop. Soon the car stopped and I decided to stop too. I turned around and it was my sister Grace and her husband Heaven. She asks me if I want to go with her and I said yes. So I ran back to the house and let my uncles and my cousins know that I

am going to leave with my sister. I know that day was sad to them because I'm leaving but me, I was so happy that I am going with my sister. My mind was still little at the time, and I didn't know that I am going to face a different life. The different I'm talking about is very shameful. But anyways things happen for a reason. I believe everything that's happening right now is t make every human learn the life and why we here.

"Why I Know She Is My Sister"

I stayed in Whisper Village with my mother, step-father, sisters, and my brothers. I love my family with all of me, and I respect them too. The love that I have for my village, I could not explain. The whole village knows my mom and the way she act. My mom was the best mother that no one could ask for. The way I saw mother serve her husband was like serving the king. My step-father is a carpenter and they are both Christian people. They make a small business and that business is to sell pancake and coconut. My mother was a very strong woman. My mother and her husband play poker every night with people from other villages like Musumusu, Algae Village, Deeplow Villlage, Moon Village, Lion Village, Yellowsage Village, Dragonfly Village, Cosmic Village, and Mangry in the western islands. All the people from those different villages are all welcome in my mom's house and do whatever they want. They have been continuing doing that. The other day I see my other

siblings and myself being abused, but it a must for me to forgive my family. When I was 12 years old, my mom told us girls that we are going downtown for the flag celebration. They Flag Day was on June 1972 and that was the first flag celebration for the Samoa Independence. My mother asks us if we still remember the town and I said yes. And my mother said that place is better now than before. We were so happy and can't wait to go. We didn't sleep the whole night and was looking at the clock and wish to tick fast. About 4:30 a.m., and my mom woke us up. We were like flash that time getting ready because we can see the bus coming already. My mother was the one that prepare everything for us girl and my step-father. We went downtown for 3 days' vacation. Everything was well preparing, and so we say our good-byes to my mom and walk were the bus is at. Now the busy is on its way to Apia… (Few hours later)… We arrived to our final destination around 8am. So we went to my aunt's, and my step-father went his sister's house, and I was 12 years old at the time. At that time I didn't know I have any other siblings. After we ate breakfast that morning, everybody was talking about how things work out. I saw Rose came to my aunt's house, and I heard her saying something about my dad is back, and she was referring to me, because they said that I am my father's other half or I have my dad's face. I ask my aunt, "Who is Rose talking about?", and my aunt said, "She's talking about you Water Spirits. Once I heard them saying that, I couldn't explain how I felt at that time. The way I feel after that moment, I feel wonder and happy knowing that I have other sisters and brothers. Rose ask my aunt is she can take me with her so

I can go meet my other sister and my whole family. They were saying something to themselves, eye contacting each other and doing there sign languages to each other and I was just sitting looking at them. And lastly they told me to get ready, because I am going with Rose. So, Rose and I went to her house to meet my nieces and my nephews, and to change my clothes and dress up good to see my sister Grace. All of those movements were doing, is to get ready and go to King of wordsand the Malietoa's family meeting. And after that meeting, they are going to have a party hosting in downtown for everybody to come have fun and to get together with each other, but most of my family was in Western Lions Village. Rose took me with her to meet my father's side of the family, my sisters, and the rest of the family. Few days later, I see lots of people from different villages went to see the 2 brothers that just arrive in Apia from England. Their names are Edward and Charles. And that why we went to the 10 years Samoa Independence Flag Celebration is to see Queen Elizabeth's two sons. The night before the celebration, I was trying my best to protect myself from the evil. That same night I saw something weird that it's not right and it something that is not supposed to happen, but too late it happens already to someone but not me. Anyways the morning of the celebration, everything feels changes in me. I choose to stay with my sisters. My step-father went back to Fagaloa with Lily and Goodys. The day I saw them left, I wasn't happy about me staying, but it was the decision I make and I know things changes in last minute. And when they left, the first thing that popped up in my mind was I know my mom is coming back to get me

the next day. But it was true. The next morning she came and I have to go no matter what, I have to listen to what my mom said. I know that it hurts me but I have to do it. My mom took me with her and all this kind of things just came up out of nowhere. When we got to the house I heard my mom was saying something about my biological father and his family, and I was just sitting there crying. I have no idea why she says that about my dad. Plus she doesn't know why I didn't come back together with my sisters and my step-father. Every time I see my step-father makes me feel sick, heart broken, and scared. And I heard him saying lies to my mom, and try to make my mom beat me up. And she did the best she can. I saw her crying and she don't want my step-father to see her crying. I was in pain when I saw my mom crying, but I can't do anything. The only thing that I can do is to calm my heart and made up and idea of running away from them and go back to my sisters in town. I made up that idea of running away and go back to the town and see if I can find someone that loves me. And because I don't know how long our family is going to be like that, so it better for me to find a way out. So, instead of running away to the town, I just went straight to my grandparents' house. Now the sacrifice is done and over with. And I don't want to beat up someone. My mom didn't realize the time I beat up my friend, because she want me to follow her way or her footsteps. I called my friend hero of the jungle or hero of fishing because she knows every technique. And I know for sure almost all the people from the South Pacific Ocean and Polynesian knows how to do it too. One day I was thinking of going visit my grandparents. And so that

day finally come. So I went to my grandmother and she said that she's going to take me with her to go visit my uncle Philips Fai. After visiting my uncle, we went to Two Way House Villagesand stayed there until my grandmother get all her stuffs. Days go by, and then my grandma left to go back home and leave me in Two Way House Villageswith one of our family. Life was fast back then. I saw my cousin Tina went with her boyfriend to the boyfriend's house and I stayed home with my uncle. When I was staying with my uncle, I serve them with respect. My uncle doesn't know that I cry every night because I want to go and free my life. I can't forget the day when I was in pain and feel like im about to go black out. However, lucky thing is that my cousin helped to walk to Poutasi, and that were the hospital is at. Right when we turn right at the 3 owner to go to the hospital, and I start too fainted. The only thing I can see is 3 black lines. So I told my cousin to please pick me up and rush me to the entrance door.

Out of all these years, God never fails me. He was with me through my whole life. Whatever that happens in the past that I didn't mention, just forgive me for whatever I did. I saw him when I was 6, and I believe that he is coming back to take me home. He came back when I was 16 and came back again to me when I was 26, then he decided to send me to Cancan Islands. Then on July 8, 2017 he rewards me with a necklace or a medallion around my neck and tells me that he is rewards me with a necklace or a medallion around my neck and tells me that he is here. Believe or not, "We Are Going Home". My family including myself believe that we are going home. We follow God and obey

his 10 commadments also he showed me the way. I know it's not only me that believe in him but we have others too. I found 3 visions that matches with mine. All the people that helps me with my journey that I didn't mention their names, I just want to say thank you for helping me out. I cant give anything for a reward or appreciation but only my father in heaven that can fullfil you all. For all of you that believe in our God, let us come together and honor him and follow him in whatever he wants us to do.

"Daily Prayer"

[1] The LORD is my shepherd; I shall not want.
[2] He makes me lie down in green pastures.
He leads me beside still waters.[1]
[3] He [g]restores my soul.
He [h]leads me in [i]paths of righteousness[2]
for his [j]name's sake.
[4] Even though I [k]walk through the
valley of [l]the shadow of death,[3]
I will [m]fear no evil,
for [n]you are with me;
your [o]rod and your staff,
they comfort me.
[5] You [p]prepare a table before me
in [q]the presence of my enemies;
you [r]anoint my head with oil;
my [s]cup overflows.
[6] Surely[4] goodness and mercy[5] shall follow me
all the days of my life,
and I shall [t]dwell[6] in the house of the LORD
[u]forever.[7]

God's promise for me is found in Isaiah 60-66.

60 "Arise, shine, for your light has come,
and the glory of the LORD rises upon you.
² See, darkness covers the earth
and thick darkness is over the peoples,
but the LORD rises upon you
and his glory appears over you.
³ Nations will come to your light,
and kings to the brightness of your dawn.
⁴ "Lift up your eyes and look about you:
All assemble and come to you;
your sons come from afar,
and your daughters are carried on the hip.
⁵ Then you will look and be radiant,
your heart will throb and swell with joy;
the wealth on the seas will be brought to you,
to you the riches of the nations will come.

The Year of the LORD's Favor

61 The Spirit of the Sovereign LORD is on me,
because the LORD has anointed me
to proclaim good news to the poor.
He has sent me to bind up the brokenhearted,
to proclaim freedom for the captives
and release from darkness for the prisoners,[b]
² to proclaim the year of the LORD's favor
and the day of vengeance of our God,
to comfort all who mourn,
³ and provide for those who grieve in Zion—
to bestow on them a crown of beauty
instead of ashes,
the oil of joy
instead of mourning,
and a garment of praise
instead of a spirit of despair.
They will be called oaks of righteousness,
a planting of the LORD
for the display of his splendor.
⁴ They will rebuild the ancient ruins
and restore the places long devastated;
they will renew the ruined cities
that have been devastated for generations.
⁵ Strangers will shepherd your flocks;
foreigners will work your fields and vineyards.

Zion's New Name

62 For Zion's sake I will not keep silent,
for Jerusalem's sake I will not remain quiet,
till her vindication shines out like the dawn,
    her salvation like a blazing torch.
² The nations will see your vindication,
    and all kings your glory;
you will be called by a new name
that the mouth of the LORD will bestow.
³ You will be a crown of splendor in the LORD's hand,
    a royal diadem in the hand of your God.
⁴ No longer will they call you Deserted,
    or name your land Desolate.
But you will be called Hephzibah,[c]
    and your land Beulah[d];
for the LORD will take delight in you,
    and your land will be married.
⁵ As a young man marries a young woman,
    so will your Builder marry you;
as a bridegroom rejoices over his bride,
    so will your God rejoice over you.

God's Day of Vengeance
and Redemption

63 Who is this coming from Edom,
from Bozrah, with his garments stained crimson?
Who is this, robed in splendor,
striding forward in the greatness of his strength?
"It is I, proclaiming victory,
mighty to save."
² Why are your garments red,
like those of one treading the winepress?
³ "I have trodden the winepress alone;
from the nations no one was with me.
I trampled them in my anger
and trod them down in my wrath;
their blood spattered my garments,
and I stained all my clothing.
⁴ It was for me the day of vengeance;
the year for me to redeem had come.
⁵ I looked, but there was no one to help,
I was appalled that no one gave support;
so my own arm achieved salvation for me,
and my own wrath sustained me.

64 [h]Oh, that you would rend the
heavens and come down,
that the mountains would tremble before you!
² As when fire sets twigs ablaze

and causes water to boil,
come down to make your name known to your enemies
and cause the nations to quake before you!
³ For when you did awesome things
that we did not expect,
you came down, and the mountains trembled before you.
⁴ Since ancient times no one has heard,
no ear has perceived,
no eye has seen any God besides you,
who acts on behalf of those who wait for him.
⁵ You come to the help of those who gladly do right,
who remember your ways.

Judgment and Salvation

65 "I revealed myself to those who did not ask for me;
    I was found by those who did not seek me.
To a nation that did not call on my name,
    I said, 'Here am I, here am I.'
² All day long I have held out my hands
    to an obstinate people,
who walk in ways not good,
    pursuing their own imaginations—
³ a people who continually provoke me
    to my very face,
offering sacrifices in gardens
    and burning incense on altars of brick;
⁴ who sit among the graves
    and spend their nights keeping secret vigil;
who eat the flesh of pigs,
    and whose pots hold broth of impure meat;
⁵ who say, 'Keep away; don't come near me,
    for I am too sacred for you!'
Such people are smoke in my nostrils,
    a fire that keeps burning all day.

New Heavens and a New Earth

¹⁷ "See, I will create
new heavens and a new earth.
The former things will not be remembered,
nor will they come to mind.
¹⁸ But be glad and rejoice forever
in what I will create,
for I will create Jerusalem to be a delight
and its people a joy.
¹⁹ I will rejoice over Jerusalem
and take delight in my people;
the sound of weeping and of crying
will be heard in it no more.
²⁰ "Never again will there be in it
an infant who lives but a few days,
or an old man who does not live out his years;
the one who dies at a hundred
will be thought a mere child;
the one who fails to reach[j] a hundred
will be considered accursed.
²¹ They will build houses and dwell in them;
they will plant vineyards and eat their fruit.

Judgment and Hope

66 This is what the LORD says:
"Heaven is my throne,
and the earth is my footstool.
Where is the house you will build for me?
Where will my resting place be?
² Has not my hand made all these things,
and so they came into being?"
declares the LORD.
"These are the ones I look on with favor:
those who are humble and contrite in spirit,
and who tremble at my word.
³ But whoever sacrifices a bull
is like one who kills a person,
and whoever offers a lamb
is like one who breaks a dog's neck;
whoever makes a grain offering
is like one who presents pig's blood,
and whoever burns memorial incense
is like one who worships an idol.
They have chosen their own ways,
and they delight in their abominations;
⁴ so I also will choose harsh treatment for them
and will bring on them what they dread.
For when I called, no one answered,
when I spoke, no one listened.
They did evil in my sight

and chose what displeases me."
⁵ Hear the word of the LORD,
you who tremble at his word:
"Your own people who hate you,
and exclude you because of my name, have said,
'Let the LORD be glorified,
that we may see your joy!'
Yet they will be put to shame.

¹⁷ "Those who consecrate and purify themselves to go into the gardens, following one who is among those who eat the flesh of pigs, rats and other unclean things—they will meet their end together with the one they follow," declares the LORD.

¹⁸ "And I, because of what they have planned and done, am about to come[k] and gather the people of all nations and languages, and they will come and see my glory.

¹⁹ "I will set a sign among them, and I will send some of those who survive to the nations—to Tarshish, to the Libyans[l] and Lydians (famous as archers), to Tubal and Greece, and to the distant islands that have not heard of my fame or seen my glory. They will proclaim my glory among the nations. ²⁰ And they will bring all your people, from all the nations, to my holy mountain in Jerusalem as an offering to the LORD—on horses, in chariots and wagons, and on mules and camels," says the LORD. "They will bring them, as the Israelites bring their grain offerings, to the temple of the LORD in ceremonially clean vessels. ²¹ And I will select some of them also to be priests and Levites," says the LORD.

²² "As the new heavens and the new earth that I make will endure before me," declares the LORD, "so will your name and descendants endure.²³ From one New Moon to another and from one Sabbath to another, all mankind will come and bow down before me," says the LORD. ²⁴ "And they will go out and look on the dead bodies of those who rebelled against me; the worms that eat them will not die, the fire that burns them will not be quenched, and they will be loathsome to all mankind."

On February 8-10 2017, I saw 3 rainbows
and that is a message for us.

On July 8, 2017 my journey completed.

July 10, 2017 interview completed.

July 14, 2017 VBS finished.

August 21, 2017 during the eclipse day, we make 37,452 footsteps offer on Eagle Fall in Lake Tahoe for the world to make peace and be safe.

On September 19 2017, I slept under the unfinished chambers bridge with the poor and homeless trying to complete and make everything possible. In the midnight, Lisa and Wendell and the entire homeless people sleeping, and it was just me that went walk and pray at the same time. While I was walking I saw a north star, and I believe that my pray is answering.